# SO MANY MOVING PARTS

**Tiffany Atkinson** was born in Berlin in 1972 to an army family, and has lived in Wales since moving to Cardiff to take a PhD in Critical Theory. She now lectures in English and Creative Writing at Aberystwyth University.

She won the Cardiff Academi International Poetry Competition in 2001. Her first collection, *Kink and Particle* (Seren, 2006), a Poetry Book Society Recommendation, won the Jerwood Aldeburgh First Collection Prize and was shortlisted for the Glen Dimplex New Writers Award. *Catulla et al* (Bloodaxe Books, 2011), her second collection, was shortlisted for the Roland Mathias Poetry Award (Wales Book of the Year) in 2012 and was a *TLS* Book of the Year. Her third collection, *So Many Moving Parts* (Bloodaxe Books, 2014), is a Poetry Book Society Recommendation.

# TIFFANY ATKINSON

# SO MANY
# MOVING PARTS

BLOODAXE BOOKS

Cover design: Neil Astley & Pamela Robertson-Pearce.

Printed in Great Britain by Bell & Bain Limited, Glasgow, Scotland, on
acid-free paper sourced from mills with FSC chain of custody certification.

# ACKNOWLEDGEMENTS

Many thanks to the editors of the following publications in which some of these poems have appeared: *American British and Canadian Studies, English: Journal of Literature and Reviews, Identity Parade: New British and Irish Poets* (Bloodaxe Books, 2010), *Out of the Woods: Adventures of Twelve Hardwood Chairs* (RCA, 2012), *Poetry Review, Silk Road Review*.

I would also like to thank the Hawthornden Trust for a Residential Fellowship in 2011, Literature Wales (formerly Academi) for a Writer's Bursary in 2011, and Aberystwyth University for a semester of Research Leave in 2012. Enormous thanks to Neil Astley for his patience and encouragement, and to the Aberystwyth Poetry Workshop for good advice and friendship.

# CONTENTS

# Nightrunning

So much cold
even the moon can't swallow it
or the harbour in its fishy dark. You
balance your breath like a bowl of dry
ice. It's all a mistake, this body,
this job, this love. Somewhere inside
where the heart spins hard on its string
is an animal watching. It scratches
at night, perhaps with a beak or a tusk,
is neither kind nor unkind, just restless.

So much rain
even the deepest hill can't filter it
or the river with its open gills. You
carry your heart like a full dish of blood.
It's all such a blessing, this body,
this job, this love. Somewhere inside
where the lungs stretch their intricate wings
is an animal watching. It wriggles
at night and shows its belly or its tender scales,
is neither kind nor unkind, just restless.

# Two parts of rain

## I *Groundwater*

All day the land has been studying
books and books of water.

It has dropped off
face-down in the page.

You must walk in it.
What is the rain but a literature

you thought you had down pat
except that wasn't it, quite.

Cloud hobbles east
on its bruised foot.

Are you restless? no wonder.
Groundwater in its way is muscular

and bears in mind a huge unthinkable push.
Sometimes you don't know your own strength.

See how the leaves in their running
try even to outrun the river.

And someone's been feeding
the heart's cold pony in its claggy field.

II *The bodies of others*

Walking out from the castle
casting off stone by stone
the small town of self; ground-
water whelming the track and the rain

spinning rain. A doe and her fawn
in the loom of soaked greens are there/
not there, as something unseen in a poem
will recoil on itself like a fern

and regrow for astonishment. Down
in the thrum of the blood in the doe's
lit face in the rain in the green of a poem
upholding the leafy right to be amazed

all of us walking out see them. None
can agree whether distance or proximity
moves first in the bodies of others; and
these are still things that can happen.

# Farm Sale, Tregaron

What do they want from us,
these things; cracked harnesses,
two fat tyres in a crucible of mud,
inscrutable tilling machines, an oil-
dulled Raeburn with its bloody dish of rust?

Here is the horsebox spilling its guts,
an ancient navy Citröen with its hood up.
No one needs so many empty feed-tubs
or a gate laid flat like an old pound note;
no one will shine the pretty milk-churns.

Christ so cold, and not yet December.
*Bwys bach* but it's strange, a daughter says,
in storm apparel and dark glasses. To another,
one of five, now Mari you're the hoarder,
something you got from Dad... And all

the farms of Ceredigion send people four-
by-four; a burger-van fires its canisters,
the auctioneer rigs his windy stage. Who
for this sheepskin deep enough to make a baby
in? Who for this hay bale cradle standing true –

and each so hungry we could eat the sheepskin,
chilled enough to climb inside the bales. But
this is a passing of things: a litany of six good
milk-churns, half a working stove, the sun
in fairness touching each still life with blood.

## Animal Truck

It is only the wet road hissing.
The animal truck is passing.
Stepping off the kerb I meet
the look, direct and arterial
of calves, perhaps – too high
and wild for sheep – their eyes
pour through the slats marked
J  NES & SONS LLANDYSUL. Rain
comes gently down and eyes
slide by like a slow contraction.
The dead are among us, trailing
their cortisols down North Parade.
Behind me a child sounds a nasal
reveille. The lights are changing
and we carry our soft uninjured
bodies to classrooms and offices.
Here comes the hard rain, rinsing
the calm street and our tender shoes.

# Two moments in white

At three a.m. on the longest night
and no sleep since Monday I park
in thick wind and scoop my career
from the passenger seat in inches of
loose pages. The wind has it in for me.
Oh my nightshift oh my annotations –
what a huge magnolia in slow detonation,
what an angel, what a din of unhinged
wings. I stand in my lozenge of dark
as the wind shakes my bones. Oh. Oh.

Four hours later jogging for the train
through black streets. Who's the girl
in nothing but an origami party dress,
three sheets to the wind and silver shoes
in one hand? Slap slap slap, her damp heels
take the pavement and her skirt explodes
like spray around the dead star of her face.
What class of passenger are we, no more
solid than the wind? I turn on my spindle
all the way to Manchester. Oh. Oh.

(

what might have been said
in the night's eye's motorway caff
with one of those names
like Critchley Armageddon Services
where you propped your face
on coffee tight with sugar
and spoke of your marriage was

that sexuality is mostly a crystal
like the grit of sugar at the elbow
on a wipe-dry table or a minor abrasion
like Christmas and the coffee was good
which we stirred like people in grown-up
shoes so sweet our hands grew giddy
and the road home soft between the teeth

)

# Hex

in the striplit corridors from the water
cooler to the post-room. Something
amiss with the coffee machine: each
takes a bitter cup back to their private
archive. Back at my desk I click refresh,
refresh: no one did ever or could love me.
Sunlight clatters in and students follow
with biros and insouciance – didn't we
all wake rich in grace and blood. But
even the princess in her crystal cubicle
chews her sandwich slowly. Sometimes
ambition flares in her like a happy malaria,
sometimes she could lay right on down & die.

# Diggers

overnight have seized control
of the little roundabout. All

they want to talk about is surfaces
to any road that will listen.

I sing with my toddler godson
about the lives of large vehicles,

their yellow huge behaviours
and deep hands. They broadcast

all day through our tremulous
offices, plainsong and artillery,

old masculinity, riots and funerals,
helpless with babies and cutlery.

# Match day

I was scrubbing the kitchen
actually but heard my neighbours
next-door downstairs in the hallway
up and down the country roaring
as the game unpacked its tricks

Now sunset drives its ambulance into the sea
and town applies itself on all fours
to the drinks    Tomorrow marriages
resume their gentle topple onto rocks
and A&E will brim with casualties

But first some god has kicked our faint
hearts clean over the post and we must
grope through shot grass after them    whole
families in the same shirt    grinning dogs
and Spring    smug bastard    rooting in the stands

## The Starling Cloud

Whose god led me here, to a family pub
just opened by the railway in a clap
of chip-fat? When a train goes by the children
clamour at the fencing like a set of knives.
There's no drink strong enough. Gruff's
furry hood and Harry's pale intense face
swim from the hive of the climbing frame.
Who put them there? What shakes the red
flag of their joy, and how did I exempt myself?

# La poulette grise

*an IVF lullaby*


It's the grey chicken who lays in the church,
    hunkering down where cold dust
    hems her skirts
    little sin-eater
        She's going to lay a beautiful

It's the white chicken who lays in the branches,
    lean as a whip of willow
    in March breezes
    little dream-catcher
        She's going to lay a beautiful
        a beautiful little coco for

It's the black chicken who lays in the armoire,
    freshening the rusty silks
    for feast days
    little pearl-warmer
        She's going to lay a beautiful
        a beautiful little coco for
        her little one

It's the yellow chicken who lays in the alders
    under dropping leaves
    in shoals of rain
    little nut-warbler
        She's going to lay a beautiful
        a beautiful little coco for
        her little one who's going to
        do dodo

It's the green chicken who lays in the glazes
        soft crystal tunnels
        pecked by bees
        little seed-hatcher
                She's going to lay a beautiful
                a beautiful little coco for
                her little one who's going to
                do dodo dodiche dodo

It's the brown chicken who lays in the moon
        intuited egg of the tides
        O sin-eater dream-catcher
        pearl-warmer nut-warbler
        seed-hatcher         O
        meteorite in the piazza

                She's going to lay a beautiful
                a beautiful little coco for
                her little one who's going to
                do dodo dodiche dodo    She's
                going to lay a beautiful
                a beautiful little

# Guts

My dear friend's in purgatory
on account of his guts. IBS,
he says, plays Matthew Corbett
to his Sooty, which I googled:

fist to puppet. Ira's a philosopher
and owns he relishes humiliating
comedy. Recently my father had
a portion of his gut cut out and one

part doubled like a pinky through
his abdomen. He tackles meals
backwards from the thought of what
may pass through. He's a parable.

Once at a writers' retreat a stranger
leaned through candlelight to say
he prayed every day for his wife,
for relief from her punitive bowels;

dry pellets he said, like beech mast
or acorns, hour by hour, indignity
enough to make her weep. I thought
him drunk but he was sharp-eyed

and a kind man. Yesterday I ran
three hours on caffeine: at mile ten
I ducked beneath a bridge and squatted
like a dog in dead leaves feeling occult,

hooked up to a secret sphere of minuscule
fauna and landscapes, twenty-five feet
of watery engine churning at the river-
mouth, that dark unloved star.

# A Film of Gannets

which builds from static
resolving to ocean and atoll,
remotely unlovable. As if

by will the air becomes
gannets, an idea of geometry
pushed through a ravenous body:

think of them hour after hour
extinguishing their white flames
in the sea's cold solvents. What

a politics of fish and rock and
fish and fuck and rock. No room
for subtlety. It's a colony.

Had you forgotten the din
like heaven emptying itself
of filthy cutlery, bringing brine

to the eyes and a sense of flesh
and injury? You and I and gannets
have a complex history: in your

gallery dark I can't be sure which
foot my foot, which eye my eye,
who bird and who stung sea.

# Havisham

By then I'd used so little of myself
my voice was cracked, my muscles
dragged, my breasts had crawled

inside my chest. I left the phone
to wither on its vine and drifted
in my crinoline of stink from room

to room. It was in fact a quaintly
restful time, almost Victorian you
might have said, being American;

indeed I'd nearly looped my throat
with jet and hooked my crystal coffin
to its coach and horses when I met

the girl you clamoured at. No sir,
my tiny mother did not push me
from the dark for that. My father

did not graft all day of fifty years
for that. And you, you were a glitter
by the roadside, glimpsed at speed,

en route by god to some town boasting
opera, balls and all five major super-
markets, ruinous casinos and its own zoo.

# Barstool, by Michael Warren

Out of the woods comes
the hand and its delicate fretwork;
how little a man needs
to carry his weight in the end.

Perhaps it's a dud summer
and rain has run all afternoon
the white length of his forearm;
perhaps he is sickened or lost

or his house repossessed
or the world has burned down
to a barrow of ashes and bone
or the guests have rolled up

unexpected in breakable outfits
and there is nowhere safe to sit.
Quickened with need he will crib
from the compound tense of wood

a single unfoldable rune for still
flight, one for each soul in its
hobble of flesh; and this is how
whole new cities flower overnight.

# Solar

Huswifely
sun of the busy
hands and mandibles

peck out my shadows
and name me afresh     Set
me upright     Pull the ripcord

of my heart so it spins like a seed in the wind
then switch on the skin's net of lights
and push me out in just what I stand up in

Spare me a slow death's chills and bruising
and let me not cower and cling     Fire
the wormholes of my bones until I rise

like a Chinese lantern     Mark me for danger
and blaze and broadcast this handful of matter
since I am nobody else's child

# Crystal

First true heat of the year. I sway
in your wake through a new town

with olives and wine
and an hour between trains,

only how can we spread for each other
our delicate, separate pains

when a black lab is earthing herself,
right now, in front of the sun?

Her eyes swivel in; she's a dark blood
diamond quivering at work, a kind of eclipse.

Crystal! Crystal! calls a woman
rounding the church with a dangling lead.

Homo... homo sapiens is *shit!*
shouts the drunkard from his lock of shade.

The dog has unhinged her sticky thorn
of crap and flown, her shadow with her;

we have laughed ourselves shiny and flat.
Oh, Ira, what does the world want?

# Beachcombing

Children will enter the water hands first. There's
a knack that women all over the world have
of putting up hair in a knot, the pale nape gathers
the salt. The babushka and the magpie
own the beach but no one cares. Her fingers
strum the muscles in her thighs. She's a mountain
but her fingertips are diamonds. This patisserie
of crotches in their little wraps; how tenderly
we don't look. Airport novels crackle in the sand.
Even the baby's too dazzled to cry; his fat hands
bounce on the breeze. I have spent a half-life
on the wrong strand. Here's the barman's daughter
selling frappé. I would like a bitter chinking glassful
emptied on my head. I would like to drink the sea.
I'd like every tiny house of sand to wear me down.
When the small brown woman comes to snap the
last umbrellas shut, she'll tut and sweep the bones.

# Boy with Red Umbrella

and both of you askew
against such light. Your sunbed
drifts in a hoop of shoes: they've
left you to your anteroom of shade,
your rose-pink sister fitting her snorkel-
mask dumbly, your terrible parents
hand in hand. For the length of your limbs
you're no more a man than an orchid.
Beyond you the pleasure boats zip and
stall, the green sea thickens and glitters,
women oil and spread themselves.
Nothing has happened yet. Nothing may
ever. You gaze out stunned at the hills
with one palm pressed to the sand, as if
the earth might raise its pulse to say
it's coming, yes, it's *now*, whatever it is.

# Girl with Blue Towel

Out of the cool bar bolts the hotel's
official photographer, a surfer dude
in a lickable tan: the freckled girl
who chaperoned her high heels in
so carefully now sprints past barefoot,
maybe fourteen, striped bikini strobing
past the torpid pool and into the crackling
park where friends call *Magda* but she's
laughing, as is he, across the veldt
of maybe ten years where there isn't
much to give a sense of scale to things;
she's grabbed a huge blue towel and
in a sort of category error draped it
from her head; she sways there like a noon
ghost and could stay like that for ever so
he snaps her anyway, Saint Bartholomew
of the sunbeds, holding the culpable
skin out like a windsock; such is the body.
Perhaps he goes back to the bar to smoke
and text his girlfriend; perhaps he's a man
who knows he's set a long fuse burning back
all afternoon toward the possibility that she's
the rarest creature on the beach, a private
tartness she will worry with her tongue all
winter as she practises this walking in the skin.

# Avdimou

This is the beach from thirty years ago:
my father liked to sail from here to Greece
and live on tiny biscuits. This the swoon
of sea where one long dreamy afternoon
I held my favourite thing over the deck
and let him go. He was a soldier like
my father; I had such a fizzy passion
for his shiny buttoned chest and blunt
black hair. I held his wooden hand and
let him go. I was an odd child, everybody
said so. They were sunbathing and chewing
tiny biscuits and I had to feed the animal
of sea, with both my parents still alive
and all my friends and pets and teachers,
nothing but the blue sky and the dazzle,
dazzle of it. And I didn't cry but stared out
at his spreading wake and felt its wave
break hard against my ribs, regather,
break, for weeks. My kindly, blameless
family might have been concerned. I had
forgotten this; am not sure what it means.

# Woman with Paperback Romance

She has freed herself lately
from those hooks; her cigarette
says so and the way she snorts at each
flipped page. Let the young men detonate
across the baked sand, let them ring
the huge bell of the sea. She has the sun
for that, that keeps on, keeps on giving.
Boys, her careful wearing of dark glasses
says, get over yourselves. She balances
her backbone at the bar against a glass
of Sauvignon; in just ten days she'll land again
for rush-hour, shopping, heartbreak. What
does the dog want that howls all night,
the lizard with its soft translucent hands?

# Roaming

Darling are you – can you –
no I'll wait. Give Madison
and Grace and Eloise my love,

and don't believe me if I tell you
this is my bare hand down the U-
bend of the language, scrubbing.

No I was speaking to. Sometimes
I talk to other people you know.
Oh sweetheart, that was a joke.

Yes such a spendthrift wasn't I,
love love love. Yet here I am
three thousand or so miles away

and hooked up to the hydroponic
of a mobile phone and isn't it
simple, talking? TALKING. Darling

you are breaking up but what
I was trying to. What I was trying
to say was. Well you know how

sometimes what you want to say
is. No not that. There is a party
next door; also there's a moon

like something built by children
and a creature in the palm tree
shrieking gently. Are you still there?

Never mind, I said. Yes. Probably
next week. Perhaps it's giving birth –
I think it's female. Taxi. Or it's dying.

# The hands of flight attendants

shake us like napkins
from thin air
and place us helpless in our own laps.
How precious we are,
two hundred or so fitted gems.

They have blessed us and
rendered us so light and airworthy
they must buckle us down
for our own good
like a vestibule of hysterics.

Now they mime *over the head*
*like so* and here is the whistle and here
the tiny lantern; if that happens
we will follow Natalie's Sanjay's Astrid's
polished fingertips into the foam

and help must arrive
like a microwave dinner
from their fledged palms. Nothing
can take place that couldn't be passed
through the capable hoop of their

fingers; not the aircraft itself
and its smooth chambered tonnage
nor our small hooves kicking
as the hands whistle through us,
setting things bonelessly upright.

# Media luna

*(for J.F.)*


In the gleaming cafés
of your country I ate the new moon
over and over, always the wrong way up,
impossibly sweet. Did you think it was kind
to feed a guest so she'd be starving ever since?

Jacaranda, you told me,
the tree that combed the moon's
cool sugars out by night. That evening
I threw my crutches in the river at Rosario
and thought I shouldn't like you. I was wrong.

It took fourteen hours
of sleepless flight before the moon
could right itself. I hobbled home with green
leaves where my mouth should be, to autumn
from the petal-shattered streets of you, true south.

# Plumbing

To your flat as high and tiny
as a needle's eye the plumber climbs
twelve flights. Nothing will drain:

the kitchen and the bathroom swill
with unsolved history. Madame
next door begins her daily tattoo

on the party wall. Meanwhile
flushing the loo three times for emphasis
he says your pipes alone drain upwards.

Well. He leaves at six to meet his girlfriend
out of Mass and fuck it every pipe
despatches straight to heaven. Oh

be careful what you wish for here;
the city downstairs is already rebuilding
itself from silverware and linen.

# Old gold ring trick
*(for G.K.)*


As if in a dream
with the multiple sightlines
of dream which is Paris
and into our joined private shadow
she rises
      with sun in her hand –


*attendez, Monsieur!*
she has found something precious,
a heavy gold band and no need of it,
*pas de mari,*
      *mais vous, mais vous Madame!*


(my naked hands, your hot gaze
and the city's clinching centuries)


please, *quelque chose…?*
She mimes the hunger of herself
her complicated air-children
      and all the world


Three times we pass by
and the free streets roll with gold –
      always a woman
rising *douce et sérieuse*


half-stone-half-
sky between the couples
in their dumb stalls

# Nose

Oh the Paris perfumeries.
How did my cheap suburban brain
ever learn this arcana of roots and transparencies,

odours of sweetshops and sweatshops'
shimmering sticky gourmands
and genital civets, how a scent's

a fuse lit on the wrist making a drama
of the skin, the breeze, the whole campanile?
I've followed strangers down lift-shafts

and out of cafés into jagged streets
because their perfume rang some distant bell
or detonated chord by chord impossible

cellophane flowers... Pointlessly extravagant,
this nerve of bourgeois sensibility
that twitches through the sullen flesh, and sings.

# First communion

The body of Christ
comes down in a flurry
of fresh white collectables.

It drifts in the palm like
a flake of soap or fish

yet has been known to burn
clean through the hand
and then the whole world.

Flat and tooled and matte
and odourless, what won't it

slip through: what does it *want*
that it travels such distances
pressed and papery with hurt?

Back in the clay it is anyone's.
Doesn't it run through the woods

after any old thing with one
hell of a din and no anorak,
hunting down heaven knows what?

# Paternoster

God is big between the fingers,
bevelled like a cherry seed. First
it goes Mary / space / Mary / space/
Mary / space / Mary / space / Mary /space /

**GOD**, and when you touch this bead
a flash in his eye pulls you in
and you drift like a spaceman.
Either side Our Lady listens softly

growing lilies from her sad eyes. So
I put up my hand and said God is a mineral
Mary is vegetable and Jesus the Lamb
which is all of things, and a scientific

way to think of it, but Sister Joan
said not exactly, child. I didn't say
the paternoster is a diamond though, it
sizzles in your fingers like a diamond

feeling fiercer than it wants, or Mary
has flowers for eyes and Jesus well Jesus
did nothing but bleed his whole life; or
the space between each bead is where

you feel your hand, your weird hand
reaching in the dark like something not
yours but applied to you like names
or school reports, and sometimes

from chapel you meet yourself going
back in, a repetitive self like a little bead
pulled by the weight of the rest
asking what am I, what am I, that my

breath moves slowly in the soft dark
and I wait for god to choose, to give me
weight, the mineral pureness that'll
turn my many sides to him and dazzle.

# Ear worm

*Anon come in another man: takes off his crown,*
*kisses it, pours poison in the sleeper's ears,*
*and leaves him.*

HAMLET, III, 2

What is like earache
but the shoot of a whole lifetime's
pain in one tightening spiral:
those childhood infections
so close to the brain; my father
frightened to touch
as if pain like a hot tong
was something you couldn't put down.

Poor Hamlet, his sore otological ghost,
what a terrible ear worm: List, list,
o, list! Nights stunned soft
with opiates wouldn't have helped him
either. The brain's a tuber
spiked side-to-side with hot needles;
there is nowhere else to put it.
Speak. I am bound to hear.

## Mother,

I have spent all night
of thirty years on the windy rampart.
I have not worn my anorak
and sometimes have smoked
into such flammable sunsets
it's a wonder the sky stayed up.
I hear the page of a paperback
turned three streets away; I know
that next-door's greenfly flourish
rowdily on. Summers have shrunk
to a handful of dull coins rolling
down the drain. Perhaps you could
tell me if this is the world's end.
Perhaps you sing us all (Dad sends
best wishes) one last filthy song.

# 8 Mühlenberg Weg

Dad's gift for parenting
grew through us like a cleft stick.

He knew we needed burrows
built of darkness and our own breath;

nor did he bother us in them. Best
was the caravan's fitted republic

of bunks and a flushable loo
in whose chemical dusks

we squatted like foxes and cherished
our smells. Equally an army man

from an unbroken line of bastards
he doled out peril in proportion

to our height. My sister, the eldest,
gangly as a hand-whisk, went first

on the death-slide that dropped
from the beech tree two houses high

and swooned across our roof,
the caravan, the swarming road,

into the green lap of the roundabout.
It was the 80s; no one seemed to mind.

Next off the rampart in my sticky jeans
I heard him whooping as I sizzled down,

my brother's pale face at the skylight
like a shell in a paperweight. Yes,

we agreed, as we crapped it all out
in the knackered old van, he was a man

who loved his step-kids as his own; his
own with familiar English ambivalence.

# Female Reproductive System

What prepared us for the ram's head
sunk in the swell of our hips, good
convent girls? Sister Carmelita
in the sick bay with the overhead
projector; first the crampy blood-bag
then its frilled impedimenta – word
by word she pinned us to our choices
as we gazed into our laps: girls, girls;
no more the sweet bikini speaking
freely or the blameless belly.

# Male Reproductive System

On the second day the penis and
its sidekicks lolling like an old
doll in a folk museum; in cross-
section dangling south-westerly
like England, grainy tip forever
sloughing into spray. Small wonder,
boys, you race to catch up with your-
selves before the world drops over-
night with no more than a whisper
into deep amnesiac sea.

## Choose

Having been here before
between impossibles

like mirrors in a changing room
that whack you back and forth between yourself

until you put out your hand
or call for the glittery assistant

I am checked in by a bee and a cowgirl
since it's Halloween

inappropriate perhaps
as the bee's antennae bounce above the paperwork

and my mother's ghost
for she still enjoys the cubic poshness of hotels

asks on her way through the coffee-dark lobby
*what* am I feeding my heart on these days

that it gutters so
and cannot lift its own weight?

# On driving

as minor domestic psychosis,
like love, or credit –

the megalomanic swoon of it,
the ego kicking in its booster seat.

Guess who passed first time,
despite Dad slamming his brake-foot

through the passenger footwell
of the Volvo every Sunday afternoon

for months: it takes hours in empty carparks
for a girl to saddle up to hazard,

which isn't to say she won't learn
to love it, seeking herself at speed

by night in black rain on a jag of hair-
pin bends, per second per second

unhitching her training-wings
to feel the body's soft bud hang

like light in space. Look, daddy, look
at all the things a fast girl can let go.

# Five-finger exercise

Today we have studied your hand:
its abacus of small bones
reckoning,

how light breaks through the prism
of your fingers, antique roses
on the back's

smacked saddle. We have walked
your palm this quiet afternoon,
its genteel

districts, buffed the knuckles' pebbles
and sampled the intimate waxes of
your fingernails,

the nipply pink of the tip of the muscular
thumb and each joint's wrinkly
gearbox,

five gold rings in order of weight,
the wrist's pale flag above the whip-
crack wrist-bone

gathering each copper-bottomed vein,
and ours is the lunar distance
of a hand unheld.

Yet what is this family but a boom town
hatched of the hand, your hand in its dumb
bud, dreaming?

# On crying

being not sadness exactly,
which as you know has slow,
deep flesh like any large mammal
and mostly lies close where you left it;

while tears in themselves are amphibious,
fickle, lunar, flash-in-the-pan,
the watery double upsetting the dish.
To wit, and filling out the usual forms, etc

I am awash, and such a show of scales
and iridescence. Don't ask – one might
just as well weigh rainbow – and besides,
I don't know. Nonetheless

I hold the brimming thing to you,
good grief, at our age, this clay bowl
of minerals and all our common waters.
This is what we're really made of. Drink.

## Phallus Impudicus
*(for R.S.)*


That clarion stink. A death. Schlong-shroom! says Phil,
who spots it mooning through the tree-roots. The stink-
horn is hysterical with flies. Rebecca
    sickens with a sting

that overnight grows like a rose and all its
thorns across the right side of her face. Inside
the shady castle she turns softly on her
    histamines. Meanwhile

we itch for Coke and salty snacks and fall too
often into innuendo. One may talk
from seven p.m. Writing life is passive
    aggressive perhaps;

our loves and children have been disappointed
quietly in our quiet selfishness by
slow degrees, or not, and thrive on anyway
    despite, without us.

Given a month of outrageous privacy
what a mouthy collection of cells I am.
You wouldn't believe the stink of my exact
    indelible pains,

like the crab-juice that dripped through a paperback
during the long bus ride up. Murakami
I think. We have thrown him over the ramparts,
    unread; even so.

The stinkhorn has finished itself off and left
bare earth. It seems improbable like dream-sex,
though we heard its pale hoot travel the darkness –
     such a way to go.

## Mantra

The ego's a mistake
broader than Texas: you can drive
all day and still be neighbours, though
they say you shouldn't start from here

The ego's a mistake
with a finely tuned appreciation
of nicotine and Sancerre

The ego's a mistake
but an electric cockpit
nonetheless, boys, boys

      a mistake
though you marry it over and over
to your own noise

The ego's a mistake
that runs on good days twenty
hot miles on its own grease

      a mistake
in sixteen shades of lipstick
and a blonder person's dress

The ego's a mistake
like a wasp in a bottle

The ego's a mistake
with the horns and hooves
of a night truck of cattle

The ego's a mistake
that writes into the night
and puts in overtime
and talks if need be to the bloody document
and god deserves promotion

The ego's a mistake
that dances in the kitchen

The ego's a mistake
beneath the duvet after clocking-
in time still in Saturday's mascara
picking through old letters

       a mistake
flash-lit with hormone
like all creatures

The ego's a mistake
that turns up Mozart's *Requiem* so loud
the long-stemmed glasses in the cupboards
shake for lost friends

The ego's a mistake
that spends spends spends

The ego's a mistake
in ratios of roughly one part kiss
to four parts silence

The ego's a mistake
sharp with grievance

      a mistake
in four half-fluent languages
not including body: what a scrum –
so many moving parts

The ego's a mistake
by way of mostly false
starts

The ego's a mistake
save for itself

The ego's a mistake
hence love
hence grief